U.S. WOMEN'S TEAM

SOCCER CHAMPIONS!

Abbeville Press Publishers
New York · London

A portion of the proceeds from this book are donated to the **Hugo Bustamante AYSO Playership Fund**, a national scholarship program to help ensure that no child misses the chance to play AYSO Soccer. Donations to the fund cover the cost of registration and a uniform for a child in need.

Text by Illugi Jökulsson

For the original edition
Design: Óafur Gunnar Guðlaugsson
Layout: Ólafur Gunnar Guðlaugsson and Árni Torfason

For the English-language edition
Editor: Nicole Lanctot
Production manager: Louise Kurtz
Layout: Ada Rodriguez
Copy editor: Amy K. Hughes

PHOTOGRAPHY CREDITS

Getty Images: p. 2 (Jamie Sabau), 4 (Jonathan Daniel), 8 (Jed Jacobsohn), 10–11 (Popperfoto), 11 (Illustration: Topical Press Agency), 11 (Dick, Kerr's Ladies: Popperfoto), 12 (Andy Lyons), 15 (Tommy Cheng/AFP), 16 (Tommy Cheng/AFP), 18 (David Cannon/Allsport), 21 (Robert Beck), 22 (George Tiedemann), 24 (Peter Read Miller), 26 (George Tiedemann), 29 (Al Tielemans), 30–31 (Al Bello), 31 (Paul Hawthorne), 32 (Guang Niu), 33 (Milbrett: George Tiedemann), 35 (Goh Chai Hin/AFP), 36 (Jamie Squite), 38 (Michael Regan), 40 (Francisco Leong/AFP), 42 (Mitchell Leff), 43 (Stuart Franklin), 45 (Brett Carlsen), 47 (Leroux: Jamie Sabau), 49 (Doug Pensinger), 52 (Simon Bruty), 53 (Hollbeke: Kevin C. Cox), 54 (Jonathan Ferrey), 55 (Sauerbrunn: Grant Halverson), 57 (Marta: Michael Regan), 58 (Stephen Simpson)

Wikimedia Commons: p. 33 (Foudy: RyanDowIMG), 33 (Fawcett: Johnmaxmena2), 46 (Rodriguez: Ampatent), 47 (Press: Noah Salzman), 48 (Cheney: Ampatent), 48 (Heath: Pierre-Yves Beaudouin), 50 (Rapinoe: Jay Solomon), 51 (O'Reilly: Ampatent), 51 (Boxx: Ampatent), 53 (Cox: JMR_Photography), 53 (O'Hara: Ampatent), 55 (Krieger: Hobgoodc), 55 (Klingenberg: Ampatent), 55 (Engen: Ailura), 57 (Kawasumi: Christopher Johnson)
Árni Torfason: p. 56

First published in the United States of America in 2015 by Abbeville Press, 137 Varick Street, New York, NY 10013

First published in Iceland in 2014 by Sögur útgáfa, Fákafen 9, 108 Reykjavík

Please note: This book has not been authorized by members of the U.S. national women's team or persons associated with them.

First edition
10 9 8 7 6 5 4 3 2 1

ISBN 978-0-7892-1215-3

Library of Congress Cataloging-in-Publication Data available upon request

For bulk and premium sales and for text adoption procedures, write to Customer Service Manager, Abbeville Press, 137 Varick Street, New York, NY 10013, or call 1-800-ARTBOOK.

Visit Abbeville Press online at www.abbeville.com.

CONTENTS

Brandi Chastain of the United States celebrates with her teammates after scoring the winning goal in the 1999 Women's World Cup final against China at the Rose Bowl in Pasadena, California. The final score was 5–4.

CHASING THE DREAM

The U.S. women's national soccer team was the champion of the first FIFA* Women's World Cup tournament, which was held in 1991. Eight years later, the women from the United States won another and no less famous victory at the 1999 World Cup. The U.S. team has maintained its position as one of the world's strongest women's teams over the past 15 years. The team won the gold medal in three consecutive Olympic Games: 2004, 2008, and 2012. Furthermore, the team is ranked first according to FIFA, a position it has held since 2005.

However, Team USA has struggled while trying to obtain a third World Cup title. The women are determined, though, to make a go of it at the 2015 World Cup in Canada and take home the elusive title. The team has never been stronger—it has a collection of powerful individuals, but it is first and foremost a strong and consistent whole. The dream of the third World Cup title is therefore close to becoming a reality.

WORLD CUP 1991

WORLD CUP 1999

🔘 **OLYMPIC CHAMPION 1996**

🔘 **OLYMPIC CHAMPION 2004**

🔘 **OLYMPIC CHAMPION 2008**

🔘 **OLYMPIC CHAMPION 2012**

* International Federation of Association Football. See Glossary, page 60.

IN THE BEGINNING

Since time immemorial, some form of football has been played in most parts of the world. Various kinds of ball games played in medieval Britain developed into what we now call soccer in the middle of the 19th century. In 1863, the Football Association was established in London, England, and soon published standardized rules for the game. Over the next few decades soccer spread around Europe, and by 1900 it had become the most popular sport on the continent. Soccer then began its vigorous colonization of America and other parts of the world.

WHY "SOCCER"?

In Britain the new sport was simply called "football." Most countries use a simple literal translation of the word as their name for the sport. Given that another type of football, based on the English game of rugby, was already popular in the United States when this new sport hit its shores, Americans dubbed the latecomer "asSOCiation football," which then morphed into "soccer." The sport that Americans know as "football" is generally called "American football" in other countries.

WOMEN START KICKING

In Britain, women began playing soccer just before the turn of the 20th century. The first women's soccer game took place in 1895, in a match between teams from northern and southern England. Many women's teams were established in the beginning of the 20th century and met with vast popularity. A great number of people attended the women's soccer matches, which were generally held in order to raise funds for charity.

A women's soccer league was in the process of being established and professional soccer seemed likely. Then, in 1920, 53,000 people paid admission to watch a women's soccer match in Liverpool. In response to the huge turnout, the Football Association put its foot down and denied women access to its fields. The association asserted, "The game of football is quite unsuitable for females and should not be encouraged."

Historians claim the ban was a result of the men's worry that women's soccer was gaining more popularity. The ban did not do away with women's soccer but it did impede the development of the game for decades. Women's soccer also struggled with similar limitations in other countries. Everywhere, men viewed women's soccer with suspicion.

The Theatrical Ladies played a match at Tottenham, North London, in 1912.

Pencil drawing of
a women's soccer
game in 1895.

Dick, Kerr's Ladies football team
was founded in 1912.

Michelle Akers during a game in 1995, 10 years after she scored her first goal for the U.S. team.

THE FIRST GAMES

Women's soccer received little attention in the United States until late in the 20th century. Girls played soccer in physical-education classes, and the popularity of the sport grew slowly. Women's soccer was officially acknowledged in 1972, when Title IX of the U.S. Education Amendments was passed. According to Title IX, schools were to ensure equality for the genders in relation to education, and this of course also included sports. Schools were therefore required to equally bolster men's and women's soccer. But women's soccer still wasn't properly recognized for another decade, although from elementary schools to high schools, girls were increasingly taking to the fields. Brown University in Providence, Rhode Island, was the first college to grant full varsity-level status to its women's soccer team. Intercollegiate and regional tournaments and finally national tournaments were held.

In the early 1980s, talks began about starting a women's national soccer team. The road toward a national team was rocky, but in the summer of 1985 about 70 female soccer players gathered in Baton Rouge, Louisiana, for the U.S. Olympic Festival. It was the first time women's soccer was included in the event. The U.S. Soccer Federation hired Coach Mike Ryan to choose a national team from among the enthusiastic players gathered in the Louisiana bayou.

After the festival, the new team headed to Italy to compete against three strong European teams in the Mundialito (Little World Cup) women's tournament. On August 18, 1985, in the beautiful resort town of Jesolo, near Venice, the U.S. national team played its first official match, losing 0–1 to Italy. In the next match, the U.S. team got its first goals, in a 2–2 draw with Denmark. Two losses followed, 1–3 against England and 0–1 in another game against Denmark.

The U.S. team strengthened and grew quickly, and its performance at the 1991 World Cup clearly showed that it had become one of the world's most powerful women's soccer teams.

THE FIRST GOALS

The U.S. team's first goals were scored in a 2–2 draw with Denmark on August 21, 1985. Both Emily Pickering and Michelle Akers scored, though it is uncertain which player was responsible for the first goal. It was more likely Akers, who went on to become a legend of U.S. women's soccer.

GOLD FOR GUTS

The final game of the first Women's World Cup, held in 1991, was strenuous and competitive, but the U.S. team finally achieved a well-deserved victory over Norway. April Heinrichs, the U.S. captain, claimed that her team might lack "the sophistication and the subtlety of the European players who grew up watching soccer on TV" but made up for it "with speed, guts, and determination."

Even though the U.S. team's victory gained vast international attention, Americans themselves were barely aware of the achievement. When the team returned home with the gold, a "crowd" of around dozen people and three reporters greeted them. However, their fame would grow!

1991 Women's World Cup Final
November 30
Tianhe Stadium, Guangzhou, China
Attendance: 63,000

USA VS. NORWAY

2–1

GOALS

| USA: Akers 20' | Norway: Medalen 29' |
| Akers 78' | |

USA's Lineup
Harvey (goalkeeper)
Higgins – Biefeld – Werden – Hamilton
Hamm – Foudy – Lilly
Heinrichs – Akers – Jennings

Coach: Anson Dorrance

Michelle Akers-Stahl, who scored two goals
for the U.S. to win the first Women's World
Championship (which later became the
Women's World Cup) on November 30, 1991,
holds the trophy with teammates Julie Foudy
and Carin Jennings.

American striker Carin Jennings dribbles up the pitch during a semifinal match against Germany in Guangzhou stadium on November 27, 1991, at the first FIFA world championship for women's football.

1991 Women's World Cup
November 16–30
Host: China

Date	Opponent	Result		US Goals
Nov. 17	Sweden	3–2	●	Jennings 2, Hamm
Nov. 19	Brazil	5–0	●	Heinrichs 2, Jennings, Akers, Hamm
Nov. 21	Japan	3–0	●	Akers 2, Gebauer
Nov. 24	Chinese Taipei	7–0	●	Akers 5, Foudy, Biefield
Nov. 27	Germany	5–2	●	Jennings 3, Heinrichs 2
Nov. 30	Norway	2–1	●	Akers 2

Forward Carin Jennings was chosen the tournament's MVP, winning the Golden Ball award. With 10 goals, Michelle Akers was the leading goalscorer of the U.S. team and of the tournament, for which she won the Golden Shoe.

THE TRIPLE-EDGED SWORD IN CHINA

Only six years after playing in its first international match, the U.S. national team won a victory at the first Women's World Cup, held in China in 1991. The U.S. Soccer Federation was fantastically supportive of the women. In China, the team was led by the strong-minded captain April Heinrichs, who played in the forward position along with Carin Jennings and Michelle Akers. The three were so fierce in their scoring and assists that they were dubbed the U.S. team's "triple-edged sword." In the group stage, the U.S. women overcame all obstacles, and in the semifinals managed to win a confident victory over the European champions, Germany.

The U.S. team failed to defend its title at the 1995 World Cup. The tournament took place in Sweden, and Norway avenged its 1991 defeat in China and beat the U.S. team 1–0 in the semifinals. The Norwegian team ultimately won the cup, defeating Germany in the final.

In the 1996 Summer Olympics in Atlanta, the U.S. women made no mistakes. New players had joined the team, which clearly aimed for stronger unity among its members. The United States achieved the first goal in the final against the extremely powerful Chinese team, and then managed to weather a Chinese storm. China could only equalize the score before the Americans landed a late and deserved winning goal.

Gold! 1996

Summer Olympics
Atlanta, GA

Date	Opponent	Result		US Goals
July 21	Denmark	3–0	●	Venturini, Hamm, Milbrett
July 23	Sweden	2–1	●	Venturini, MacMillan
July 25	China	0–0	○	
July 28	Norway	2–1*	●	Akers, MacMillan
August 1	China	2–1	●	MacMillan, Milbrett

* After extra time

1996 Olympics Final

August 1
Sanford Stadium, Atlanta, GA

USA VS. CHINA

2–1

GOALS

USA: MacMillan 19'   China: Sun Wen 32'
Milbrett 68'

USA's Lineup
Scurry (goalkeeper)
Fawcett – Chastain – Overbeck
Lilly – Foudy – Venturini – MacMillan
Hamm (Jennings 89') – Akers –
Milbrett (Roberts 71')

Coach: Tony DiCicco

Team USA celebrates its win over Norway, 2–1, in the finals of the 1996 Olympic Games in Athens, Georgia.

ATLANTA GOLD!

GLORY!

This photograph of Brandi Chastain celebrating after she scored the deciding penalty kick against China in the 1999 Women's World Cup in Pasadena, California, is one of the most iconic images in women's sports. Of course, soccer players are not supposed to remove their shirts on the field, but Chastain was hardly apologetic afterward: "Momentary insanity, nothing more, nothing less. I wasn't thinking about anything. I thought, 'This is the greatest moment of my life on the soccer field.'"

The iconic photo of Brandi Chastain in 1999.

BRANDI CHASTAIN
Born 1968 in San Jose, CA
With the national team 1988–2004
Games: 192
Goals: 30

Mia Hamm in action.

TO THE FINAL

The fact that the 1999 FIFA Women's World Cup was held in the United States was a clear sign of the growing popularity of women's soccer, boosted by the Olympic gold medal in the 1996 Atlanta games. The final would turn out to be the most-attended women's sports event in history.

The U.S. team sailed safely through the tournament's group stage. The team was a strong whole, but at the same time populated by tremendously talented individuals. Mia Hamm was at her best, Michelle Akers was still at the top of her game, and players such as Kristine Lilly and Tiffeny Milbrett gained admiration for their skill and zeal. A true marker of the U.S. team's strength was a match against Germany in the quarterfinals. Twice the Germans took the lead, and twice the U.S. team equaled the score. Finally defender Joy Fawcett scored—the most important goal of her career—and ensured a U.S. victory. In the semifinals, the American women overcame the mighty Brazilians, which led to a faceoff with China in the final.

1999 Women's World Cup
Host: USA

Date	Opponent	Result		US Goals
June 19	Denmark	3–0	●	Hamm, Foudy, Lilly
June 24	Nigeria	7–1	●	OG*, Hamm, Milbrett 2, Lilly, Akers, Parlow
June 27	North Korea	3–0	●	MacMillan, Venturini 2
July 1	Germany	3–2	●	Milbrett, Chastain, Fawcett
July 4	Brazil	2–0	●	Parlow, Akers
July 10	China	0–0	5–4** ●	

* Own goal by a Nigerian player.
** 0–0 after extra time; 5–4 after penalty shootout.

Briana Scurry, Brandi Chastain, Carla Overbeck, Michelle Akers, and Mia Hamm were all selected to the tournament's all-star team. Tiffeny Milbrett was the U.S. team's leading scorer

BRIANA SCURRY
Born 1971 in Minneapolis, MN
With the national team 1994–2008
Games: 173
Shutouts: 71

A TOUGH FINAL

Vast tensions surrounded the 1999 World Cup final between the United States and China. Both teams played cautiously and failed to create proper opportunities for scoring. After 90 minutes, the game went into extra time, and fans of the U.S. team were justifiably anxious. The Chinese player Fan Yunjie came dangerously close to scoring with a header, but Kristine Lilly came to the defense at the very last moment. The scoreless game went on, and after 120 minutes the penalty shootout ensued. The score quickly reached 2–2. The Chinese failed with their third shot, but then each team scored two more. It was clear that if Brandi Chastain landed the final penalty shot, the U.S. women would become world champions. And so she did, drawing wild cheers from the crowd! Public interest in the tournament was great, a big difference from the World Cup eight years earlier.

1999 Women's World Cup Final

July 10
Rose Bowl, Pasadena, CA
Attendance: 90,180

USA VS. CHINA

0–0 (5–4*)

* After extra time and penalty shootout.

USA's Lineup
Scurry (goalkeeper)
Overbeck – Chastain – Fawcett – Sobrero
Akers (Whalen 91') – Hamm – Lilly – Foudy
Parlow (MacMillan 57') – Milbrett (Venturini 115')

Coach: Tony DiCicco

MICHELLE

Michelle Akers is the embodiment of the U.S. team during the first 15 years of its existence: powerful, physically strong, goal-driven, and cunning. These qualities have continued to characterize the team, which has added dexterity and technical skill. Not that Akers lacked technical skill—quite the contrary. She was so skillful that Pelé himself chose Akers and Mia Hamm as the only American representatives (male or female) on the FIFA 100, a list of the 125 greatest living soccer players. And in 2000, Akers and Sun Wen of China were selected by FIFA as Female Players of the Century.

Akers is the only player to have scored five goals* in a single game during a World Cup final tournament, a feat she accomplished in 1991 when the United States defeated Chinese Taipei 7–0. Akers said afterward: "Five goals in one game, what soccer player expects that? But I thought I'd take every chance I had and score every goal I can and use whatever I have to help our team be the best in the world."

* Five other U.S. women have scored five goals in a match but not in an important final tournament. See page 46.

MICHELLE AKERS
Born 1966 in Santa Clara, CA
With the national team 1985–2000
Games: 153
Goals: 105

GOLD! 2004 Summer Olympics
Athens, Greece

Date	Opponent	Result		US Goals
Aug. 11	Greece	3–0	●	Boxx, Wambach, Hamm
Aug. 14	Brazil	2–0	●	Hamm, Wambach
Aug. 17	Australia	1–1	○	Lilly
Aug. 20	Japan	2–1	●	Lilly, Wambach
Aug. 23	Germany	2–1*	●	Lilly, O'Reilly
Aug. 26	Brazil	2–1*	●	Tarpley, Wambach

* After extra time.
US top scorer: Abby Wambach, four goals

GOLD IN ATHENS

The U.S. team lost against Norway in the final of the 2000 Summer Olympics in Sydney, Australia. In the 2003 World Cup, the U.S. women played fantastically on their home field and seemed to be on the road to victory. However, they faced a harrowing defeat in the semifinals at the hands of the eventual winners, Germany. The team was forced to settle for the bronze medal in that tournament but went on to play flawlessly at the 2004 Summer Olympics in Athens, Greece. In the final against a breathtaking Brazilian team, the U.S. team displayed its might. The "famous five" (Hamm, Chastain, Fawcett, Foudy, and Lilly), who had participated since before the 1991 World Cup, still played with energy and fighting spirit. And the up-and-coming goal-scoring machine Abby Wambach eventually scored the winning goal against Brazil with a thundering header.

Abby Wambach is overcome with joy after scoring the winning goal in extra time against Brazil. Julie Foudy celebrates with her.

August 26
Karaiskaki Stadium, Piraeus

USA VS. BRAZIL
2–1*

* After extra time.
GOALS
USA: Wambach 112'   Brazil: Pretinha 73'

USA
Scurry (goalkeeper)
Markgraf – Rampone – Chastain (Whitehill 61') – Fawcett
Tarpley (O'Reilly 91') – Foudy – Boxx
Hamm – Wambach – Lilly

Coach: April Heinrichs

MIA HAMM

Mia Hamm was the face of women's soccer for 15 years and inspired numerous young girls to take up the game. Hamm's father was a U.S. Air Force colonel, who fell in love with soccer when he was stationed for a time in Italy. When the family relocated to Texas, Bill Hamm offered his six children a choice. They could either play soccer or start ballet lessons with their mother, Stephanie, a retired dancer. Mia tried ballet for a while but soon decided she preferred soccer! At first she had to play with boys' teams because she was the only girl who played in her school. Her talents developed quickly, and at the age of 15 she played her first game with the U.S. women's national team. Hamm became an enthralling forward with many talents and still remains the youngest player ever on the national team.

When Hamm was only 19 years old she helped her team win the 1991 World Cup title, and she was the driving force eight years later when the team claimed the title at the 1999 World Cup. Hamm retired, along with a few other players, following the victory at the 2004 Summer Olympics. She was just 33 at the time and could well have played full steam ahead into the foreseeable future.

FIFA named Hamm as the first women's World Player of the Year in 2001 and gave her the award again a year later. When Hamm retired, no soccer player of any nationality, man or woman, had scored as many goals as she had. However, Abby Wambach managed to beat the record in 2013. Hamm is in third place on the list of most international games played, after her U.S. women's national team companions Kristine Lilly and Christie Rampone.

Mia Hamm of Team USA walks on the field during a game against China at the Giants Stadium in East Rutherford, New Jersey. China defeated the United States 2–1.

MIA HAMM
Born 1972 in Selma, AL
With the national team 1987–2004
Games: 275
Goals: 158

Members of the 1996 Olympic gold-medal-winning U.S. women's national team, Julie Foudy, Brandi Chastain, Mia Hamm, Kristine Lilly, and Joy Fawcett, pose with Hillary Rodham Clinton (center), while they attend the premiere of the HBO Sports film *Dare to Dream: The Story of the U.S. Women's Soccer Team*, on November 29, 2005, in New York City.

A loyal member of the U.S. team for 24 years, Lilly is the most capped soccer player in the sport's history. A tricky attacking midfielder and sometime striker, she still holds third place on the list of the U.S. team's top goalscorers.

KRISTINE LILLY
Born 1971 in New York, NY
With the national team 1987–2010
Games: 352
Goals: 130

After the victory at the 2004 Summer Olympics, a few legends left the U.S. team and retired from soccer, leaving behind lasting legacies and memories of fantastic performances for their country. Kristine Lilly carried on for another six years, which is not surprising given her unconquerable fighting spirit.

LEGENDS

JULIE FOUDY
Born 1971 in San Diego, CA
With the national team 1987–2004
Games: 271
Goals: 45

An accomplished midfielder, Foudy set up numerous goals for her teammates during the golden era of the 1999 World Cup–winning team.

JOY FAWCETT
Born 1968 in Inglewood, CA
With the national team 1987–2004
Games: 239
Goals: 27

Goals are not enough to win games. You also have to prevent the other side from scoring. And that's where defender Joy Fawcett stepped in!

TIFFENY MILBRETT
Born 1972 in Portland, OR
With the national team 1991–2006
Games: 204
Goals: 100

To average a goal in every other game, as Milbrett accomplished, is no easy feat!

The 2007 World Cup in China turned out to be heavily disappointing for the U.S. team. Kristine Lilly was the sole remainder of the old guard, but with Abby Wambach on the field, the team appeared likely to succeed. However, in the semifinal match against Brazil, the U.S. team collapsed and lost, 0–4. The team received the bronze medal after defeating Norway, though it was not much compensation. No one knew what to expect in the Summer Olympics in China the following year—especially since Lilly was absent on maternity leave and Wambach was injured. But the new coach, Pia Sundhage, of Sweden, formed a strong team, emphasizing passing and technique. The women lost their first match but then steadily strengthened, culminating with a victory in the final, when the U.S. team finally took revenge on Brazil. In the absence of Wambach, it was time for other players to shine.

Heather O'Reilly scored important goals, Natasha Kai ensured victory over the strong Canadian team in the quarterfinals, and Angela Hucles was the U.S. team's top goalscorer, a great feat given that she had been a bit player for several years. Hope Solo managed a number of great saves when the team faced the superbly talented Brazilians. Yet, it was Carli Lloyd who ultimately secured the gold medal, with an awesome shot from outside the penalty area during extra time.

Gold! 2008 Summer Olympics
Beijing, China

Date	Opponent	Result		US Goals
Aug. 6	Norway	0–2	●	
Aug. 8	Japan	1–0	●	Lloyd
Aug. 12	New Zealand	4–0	●	O'Reilly, Rodriguez, Tarpley, Hucles
Aug. 15	Canada	2–1*	●	Hucles, Kai
Aug. 18	Japan	4–2	●	Hucles 2, Chalupny, O'Reilly
Aug. 21	Brazil	1–0*	●	Lloyd

* After extra time.
US top scorer: Angela Hucles, four goals

Carli Lloyd of Team USA celebrates after clinching a 1–0 win over Brazil in the Summer Olympic Games in Beijing, China, on August 21, 2008.

2008 Olympics Final
August 21
Workers Stadium, Beijing
Attendance: 51,612

USA VS. BRAZIL
1–0

GOALS
USA: Lloyd 96'

USA's Lineup
Solo (goalkeeper)
Markgraf – Rampone – Mitts
Tarpley (Cheney 71') – O'Reilly (Kai 101') – Lloyd –
Chalupny – Boxx
Rodriguez (Cox 120') – Hucles

Coach: Pia Sundhage

GOLD IN BEIJING

Abby Wambach missed the 2008
Olympics because of an injury. In
London, she was determined to do
her best for the team.

FLYING THE FLAG

In the 2011 World Cup final, the U.S. team was considered more likely to win than the Japanese team. However, the United States lost after the penalty shootout. As a result, it became ever more important for the U.S. team to defend its 2008 Olympic title at the Summer Olympics in London. The U.S. women played with great vigor and ingenuity, inspired by Coach Sundhage. In the group stage, when the United States was trailing 0–2 after only 14 minutes against the fierce French team, the U.S. women's strength clearly manifested itself, and the tide turned: Team USA finally won, 4–2. Abby Wambach and newcomer Alex Morgan had striking chemistry up front. The significance of the young and lightning-quick Morgan came to the fore in the semifinal match against Canada. Following extra time, the clash toughened, and Canadian Christine Sinclair achieved a hat trick (three goals in one game). But once injury time was reached, Morgan made the goal that shot the U.S. team into the final.

Gold! 2012 Summer Olympics
London, UK

Date	Opponent	Result		US Goals
July 25	France	4–2	●	Wambach, Morgan 2, Lloyd
July 28	Colombia	3–0	●	Rapinoe, Wambach, Lloyd
July 31	North Korea	1–0	●	Wambach
Aug. 3	New Zealand	2–0	●	Wambach, Leroux
Aug. 6	Canada	4–3*	●	Rapinoe 2, Wambach, Morgan
Aug. 9	Japan	2–1	●	Lloyd 2

* After extra time.
US top scorer: Abby Wambach, five goals

Lauren Cheney and Megan Rapinoe of Team USA celebrate after defeating Japan by a score of 2–1 to win the women's gold-medal match at the London Olympic Games at Wembley Stadium, August 9, 2012.

USA VS. JAPAN
2–1
GOALS

USA: Lloyd 8'   Japan: Ogimi 63'
Lloyd 58'

USA's Lineup
Solo (goalkeeper)
O'Hara – Rampone – Buehler (Sauerbrunn 80') –
LePeilbet
Heath – Boxx – Lloyd – Rapinoe (Cheney 57')
Morgan – Wambach

Coach: Pia Sundhage

THIRD GOLD IN A ROW

The U.S. team exhibited great determination by beating the skillful Japanese team in the final in London. Early on, Carli Lloyd scored with a strong header after Alex Morgan had set up the ball, but soon the U.S. team was in a tight spot. Lloyd scored again in the first half, this time by means of a beautiful 20-yard shot, and proved everyone wrong who doubted her presence on the team. The Japanese managed to diminish their deficit, but the U.S. team had a number of goal-scoring opportunities. The thrilling game came to a victorious end for the Americans, who claimed the Olympic gold, their third consecutive win!

RECORD BREAKERS

10 Most Capped Players

Rank	Player	Caps	Goals	Years
1	Kristine Lilly	352	130	1987–2010
2	Christie Rampone	301	4	1997–
3	Mia Hamm	275	158	1987–2004
4	Julie Foudy	272	45	1987–2004
5	Joy Fawcett	239	27	1987–2004
6	Abby Wambach	228	177	2001–
7	Heather O'Reilly	212	41	2002–
8	Tiffeny Milbrett	204	100	1992–2006
9	Kate Markgraf	202	1	1998–2010
10	Brandi Chastain	192	30	1991–2004

Top 10 Scorers

Rank	Player	Caps	Goals	Years
1	Abby Wambach	228	177	2001–
2	Mia Hamm	275	158	1987–2004
3	Kristine Lilly	352	130	1987–2010
4	Michelle Akers	153	105	1985–2000
5	Tiffeny Milbrett	204	100	1992–2006
6	Cindy Parlow	158	75	1995–2006
7	Shannon MacMillan	176	60	1994–2006
8	Carli Lloyd	181	57	2005–
9	Carin Jennings-Gabarra	117	53	1987–1996
10	Alex Morgan	77	49	2010–

Sydney Leroux (#2) and Alex Morgan (#13) celebrating.

THE COACHES

Pia Sundhage of Sweden was the team's first non-American coach, followed by Tom Sermanni, who was born in Scotland but lives in Australia. The present coach, Jillian Ellis, was born in England but has lived in the United States for a long time.

MULTIPLE CHAMPIONSHIPS

The CONCACAF Women's Championship (also called the CONCACAF Women's Gold Cup) has been held since 1991. The U.S. team has dominated this event, winning every time except 1998, when it did not participate, and 2010.

Coach	Years	Games
Mike Ryan	1985	4
Anson Dorrance	1986–1994	93
Tony DiCicco	1994–1999	119
Lauren Gregg	1997, 2000	3
April Heinrichs	2000–2004	124
Greg Ryan	2005–2007	55
Pia Sundhage	2007–2012	107
Tom Sermanni	2013–2014	23
Jillian Ellis	2014–	19*

* As of October 2014

1991
Haiti
Final April 28
USA vs. Canada 5–0

1993
USA
Final July 8
USA vs. Canada 1–0

1994
Canada
Final August 21
USA vs. Canada 6–0

2000
USA
Final July 3
USA vs. Brazil 1–0

2002
USA & Canada
Final November 9
USA vs. Canada 2–1

2006
USA
Final November 26
USA vs. Canada 2–1*
* After extra time.

2014
USA
Final October 26
USA vs. Costa Rica 6–0

THE ALGARVE CUP

The Algarve Cup is a global invitational tournament for women's national soccer teams hosted by Portugal and held annually in the Algarve region since 1994. It is one of the most prestigious women's soccer events, after the World Cup and the Olympics.

The U.S. team has competed in the Algarve Cup 19 times and won the event nine times.

THE

ABBY WAMBACH
Born 1980 in Rochester, NY
With the national team since 2001
Games: 228*
Goals: 177*

*As of December 2014

Abby Wambach at full throttle in the 2014 CONCACAF Women's Championship final on October 26, 2014. She scored four goals in the game, which concluded with a 6–0 victory by the U.S. team over Costa Rica.

GOAL MACHINE

When asked about Abby Wambach, the coach of the Icelandic women's national team was succinct: "In the box, Abby is a monster!" These words are definitely not far from the truth. Ever since Wambach joined the team she has racked up goals. On a good day she is absolutely unstoppable! Wambach has beaten most goal-scoring records. While playing in a friendly match against Korea on June 20, 2013, she scored four goals, thereby breaking Mia Hamm's U.S. national team record of 158 goals.

Bolstered by her height, physical strength, and ever-present competitive spirit, Wambach is powerful, and her headers are fantastic. Following a great performance at the 2012 Summer Olympics, Wambach was chosen FIFA World Player of the Year. Wambach has garnered numerous other awards but is still missing the World Cup gold. She will most likely not stop until she reaches that milestone!

Abby Wambach with her wife, Sarah Huffman, also a soccer player. They attended the 2013 FIFA Ballon d'Or gala in Zurich, Switzerland, on January 13, 2014. Wambach came in second place this

Because of her speed and gait, Alex used to be called "Baby Horse" when she was a rookie on the U.S. team.

ALEX MORGAN
Born 1989 in Diamond Bar, CA
With the national team since 2010
Games: 77*
Goals: 49*

* As of December 2014.

though Abby Wambach is still in her
ime, the heir to her position in the
ont line of the U.S. team has already
een named: she is Alex Morgan, who
however, first and foremost a unique
ward in her own right. Morgan is
ntning quick, outrunning most women
the field, and has a fantastic left-
ot shot. She is not only a tremendous
goalscorer, she also has a keen eye for
passes and cooperation and has assiste
numerous goals made by her teammate
Morgan is multitalented. She has writte
series of novels for young readers that a
entertaining, positive, and inspiring—no
least when it comes to soccer and sport
in general.

Alex Morgan is the author of three popular novels for and about girls
playing soccer and accomplishing their goals.

THE OFFENSE

The U.S. team is famous and feared around the world for its relentless strikers! Six U.S. players have accomplished the astonishing feat of scoring five goals in a single match, and three of those are still going strong for the U.S. team—so beware, U.S. opponents, beware!

Players Who Scored Five Goals in One Game

Name	Date	Opponent
Brandi Chastain	4/18/1991	Mexico
Michelle Akers	11/24/1991	Chinese Taipei
Tiffeny Milbrett	11/2/2002	Panama
Abby Wambach	10/23/2004	Ireland
Amy Rodriguez	1/20/2012	Dominican Republic
Sydney Leroux	1/22/2012	Guatemala

Rodriguez and Leroux held their goalfests in consecutive games during the CONCACAF Olympic qualifying tournament. Both came on at halftime and scored their five goals within only 45 minutes.

AMY RODRIGUEZ
Born 1987 in Beverly Hills, CA.
With the national team since 2005
Games: 113*
Goals: 28*

Though still young, Rodriguez is a veteran of many tournaments—and always delivers!

This young and daring striker has a Canadian mother and an American father, but early on she decided that she wanted to play for the United States. Leroux entered the national team like a comet and soon she was accumulating goals. She is both agile and industrious, she has incredible determination, and she is not afraid to throw herself into the defenders to gain the ball. Leroux and Morgan will most definitely be a ferocious striker duo on the U.S. team for many years to come.

SYDNEY LEROUX
Born 1990 in Surrey, British Columbia, Canada
With the national team since 2011
Games: 61*
Goals: 33*

An exciting newcomer to the team.

*As of December 2014

CHRISTEN PRESS
Born 1988 in Los Angeles, CA.
With the national team since 2013
Games: 32*
Goals: 15*

THE MIDFIELD

LAUREN (CHENEY) HOLIDAY
Born 1987 in Indianapolis, IN
With the national team since 2007
Games: 110*
Goals: 23*

TOBIN HEATH
Born 1988 in Basking Ridge, NJ
With the national team since 2008
Games: 81*
Goals: 11*

CARLI LLOYD

Carli Lloyd scored the winning goal for the United States at the 2008 Summer Olympics, but as the 2012 Summer Olympics in London approached, Coach Pia Sundhage was uncertain as to whether Lloyd had what it took to be a regular starter. Lloyd proved Sundhage wrong, however, much to the coach's delight! With her strength, control, and great skill in passing, Lloyd used her experience to aid the U.S. team in its march toward another Olympic triumph, incredibly scoring both U.S. goals in the final.

CARLI LLOYD
Born 1982 in Delran Township, NJ
With the national team since 2005
Games: 181*
Goals: 56*

*As of December 2014

MORE GREAT MIDFIELDERS

MEGAN RAPINOE

Megan Rapinoe is noticeable on the field with her short blonde hair, but she is particularly noteworthy for precision in passing, attack skills, and goal scoring. Rapinoe struggled with injuries in the beginning of her career, but she grew with each trial and was among the best on the team at the 2012 Summer Olympics in London. She scored three important goals, including one from a corner kick, which is very rare. She also made four assists.

MEGAN RAPINOE
Born 1985 in Redding, CA
With the national team since 2006
Games: 93*
Goals: 28*

HEATHER O'REILLY
Born 1985 in East Brunswick, NJ
With the national team since 2002
Games: 212*
Goals: 41*

SHANNON BOXX
Born 1977 in Fontanta, CA
With the national team since 2003
Games: 186*
Goals: 27*

THE CAPTAIN

CHRISTIE RAMPONE
Born 1975 in Fort Lauderdale, FL
With the national team since 1997
Games: 301*
Goals: 4*

Christie Rampone, during one of many triumphant moments, following the U.S. national team's victory over Brazil at the 2008 Summer Olympics in Beijing. She proudly holds her daughter Rylie Cate.

How long Christie Rampone will stand firm at the heart of U.S. defense is up to her. The day she turns 40—June 24, 2015—Rampone could find herself playing in the quarterfinals of the Women's World Cup, but few soccer players (male or female) last that long. Rampone contributed moderately to the efforts of the famous team that claimed the world championship title in 1999, but the following year, during the Summer Olympics she became a regular player in the and has remained in that position since. She is one of the world's mo defenders and an inspiring captain Rampone began, Michelle Akers w fiercest forward on the U.S. team; s Rampone has played with all the g stars of the women's national team

THE DEFENSE

Ekaterina Pantyukhina takes a shot, but Rache Hollebeke (in blue) com defense in a friendly ma February 13, 2014, in A

RACHEL VAN HOLLEBEK
Born 1985 in Del Mar, CA
With the national team sir
Games: 112*
Goals: 5*

STEPHANIE COX
Born 1986 in San Jose, CA
With the national team since 2005
Games: 89*

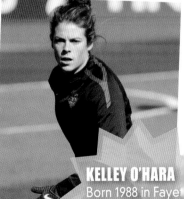

KELLEY O'HARA
Born 1988 in Fayet
With the national
Games: 49*

THE GOALIE

Hope Solo was only 19 when she played her first game for the U.S. team, which is very young for a goalkeeper. A fiery character, Hope has often courted controversy, but nobody can doubt her dedication and commitment. During the 2007 World Cup, she was benched in the semifinals, and the team then lost badly to Brazil. She openly criticized her coach for benching her and was immediately sent home from the tournament. As Solo is undoubtedly one of the best goalkeepers in the world and loves playing for her country, the rift was quickly mended, and she now holds the U.S. record for the most shutouts or "clean sheets"—games that have ended scoreless for the opponent.

HOPE SOLO
Born 1981 in Richland, WA
With the national team since 2000
Games: 159*
Shutouts: 77*

MORE DEFENDERS

Even though the U.S. team's powerful forwards are typically the most prominent players, it is no less important that the defenders be cut out for the challenge.

BECKY SAUERBRUNN
Born 1985 in St. Louis, MO
With the national team since 2008
Games: 67*

ALI KRIEGER
Born 1984 in Alexandria, VA
With the national team since 2008
Games: 53*
Goal: 1*

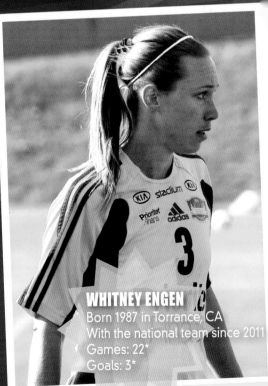

MEGHAN KLINGENBERG
Born 1988 in Pittsburgh, PA
With the national team since 2011
Games: 21*
Goals: 1*

WHITNEY ENGEN
Born 1987 in Torrance, CA
With the national team since 2011
Games: 22*
Goals: 3*

OPPONENTS AT THE WORLD CUP

GERMANY

Germany won both the 2003 and 2007 World Cups and has taken the European Championship six times in a row, a total of eight times since 1989. The German women have been tough competitors with the U.S. team for the top position on the FIFA world ranking list. Even though superstar Birgit Prinz retired after the 2011 World Cup, the German team is still packed with strong players. Goalkeeper Nadine Angerer (b. 1978) is the most famous, and her skills seem only to improve with age. She was named FIFA World Player of the Year in 2013. Nadine Kessler (b. 1988) is a budding midfielder, and the resilient Celia Šaši (a.k.a. Okoyino da Mbabi, b. 1988) is always ready to score a goal.

Nadine Angerer blocks a penalty shot from Norway during the European Championship final in Stockholm, Sweden, in 2013.

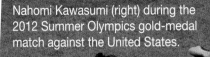
Nahomi Kawasumi (right) during the 2012 Summer Olympics gold-medal match against the United States.

SWEDEN

Pia Sundhage, who formerly coached the U.S. national team with great success, is currently at the helm of her home nation's team, and her countrywomen are already benefiting. The towering striker Lotta Schelin (b. 1984) is an unstoppable goalscorer. Nilla Fischer (b. 1984) is the glue in the steady defense.

JAPAN

Japanese women's soccer has seen much progress. Japan is currently the leading country in Asian soccer, topping the traditional powerhouses of both Koreas and China. Firm unity characterizes the team, but the offensive-minded Homare Sawa (b. 1978) is still the player to watch in a well-organized midfield. Following Japan's defeat of the U.S. team in the final of the 2011 World Cup, Sawa was named FIFA World Player of the Year. Captain Aya Miyama (b. 1985) pulls the strings in the midfield, while Nahomi Kawasumi (b. 1985) complements the play with her striking power.

BRAZIL

The Brazilian team has not reached very far in World Cup tournaments but almost invariably conquers the South American championship. If the extremely skillful goalscorer Marta (b. 1986) remains in top form, there's no telling how far Brazil may go. Marta was the FIFA World Player of the Year for five consecutive years (2006–2010) and is still at her peak. Cristiane (b. 1985) is a relentless striker on the team.

FRANCE

The French team has grown in recent years and now has a great composition of players. The team boasts the supremely gifted midfielders Louisa Nécib (b. 1987) and Camille Abily (b. 1984), who are always likely to succeed. Gaëtane Thiney (b. 1985) and Marie-Laure Delie (b. 1988) are the team's most dangerous forwards.

Marta of Brazil in action during the first round of the group stages at the London Olympic Games in a match between Cameroon and Brazil on July 25, 2012, at Millennium Stadium, Cardiff, Wales.

The future of women's soccer in the United States is very bright. Never before have so many girls played soccer, and previously unseen and ambitious efforts are being put into the country's soccer organizations. Wambach, Morgan, Lloyd, Leroux, and their companions will carry the torch for the U.S. for many years to come. However, eventually these players will leave their posts. And these eight-year-old girls will then be ready to enter the field!

THE FUTURE

Glossary

- FIFA: The International Federation of Association Football. The worldwide governing body of soccer (football), beach soccer, and futsal (indoor soccer). FIFA organizes the main international competitions, including the World Cup, for both women and men. As of 2014, 209 countries were full members of FIFA, through one of the six continental federations: AFC (Asia), CAF (Africa), CONMEBOL (South America), OFC (Oceania), UEFA (Europe) and CONCACAF.
- CONCACAF: The Confederation of North, Central American, and Caribbean Association Football [soccer]. The three North American and seven Central American associations are all full-fledged members of FIFA, but the Caribbean zone comprises 25 FIFA members and six non-FIFA territories.
- World Cup: The world championship competition of soccer, held every four years. The men's World Cup was held for the first time in 1930, won by Uruguay. As of 2014, Brazil has won five times, Germany and Italy four times each, Uruguay and Argentina twice each, and England, France, and Spain once. The women's edition was inaugurated in 1991, won by Team USA. As of 2014, the German and U.S. women's teams have won twice; Norway and Japan have won once each.

Striker: A forward player positioned closest to the opposing goal who has the primary role of receiving the ball from teammates and delivering it to the goal or assisting teammates in doing that. Alex Morgan usually assists in almost as many goals as she scores herself!

Wingers (left or right): Players who keep to the margins of the field and receive the ball from midfielders or defenders, then send it forward to the waiting strikers.

Offensive midfielder: Positioned behind the team's forwards, this player seeks to take the ball through the opposing defense and either pass to the strikers or attempt a goal herself. This position is sometimes called "number 10," in reference to the jersey number worn by the Brazilian genius Pelé, who more or less created this position.

Defensive midfielder: The DMF plays generally in front of her team's defense; her central role is to break the offense of the opposing team and deliver the ball to the forwards of her own team. The contribution of these midfielders is not always obvious, but they nevertheless play an important part in the game.

Central midfielder: The role of the central midfielder is divided between offense and defense, but mainly this player seeks to secure the center of the field for her team. Box-to-box midfielders are versatile players who possess such strength and oversight that they constantly spring between the penalty areas.

Fullbacks (left back or right back): Players who defend the sides of the field near their own goal but also dash up the field and overlap with wingers in order to lob the ball into the opponent's goal. Fullbacks are sometimes called wingbacks if they are expected to play a bigger role in the offense.

Center backs: These players are the primary defenders of their teams, and are two or three in number, depending on formation. The purpose of the center back is first and foremost to prevent the opponents from scoring, and then to send the ball toward the center.

Sweeper: The purpose of the sweeper was to keep to the back of her defending teammates and "sweep up" the ball if they happened to lose it, but also to take the ball forward. The position of the sweeper has now been replaced by defensive midfielders.

Goalkeeper: She prevents the opponents' goals and is the only player who is allowed to use her hands!

Coach:

_____

CHOOSE THE TEAM

Who do you want playing on the U.S. women's national soccer team?
Choose one goalkeeper, three defenders, four midfielders, and three
strikers. You can choose any player you want, past or present. You can
even choose yourself (as long as you are a girl) or your friends!

Goalkeeper:

_____

Right back:

_____

Left back:

_____

Defender:

_____

Defender:

_____

Midfielder:

_____

Midfielder:

_____

Midfielder:

_____

Forward:

_____

Forward:

_____

Forward:

_____

THE COACH PUTS YOU ON THE BENCH, MUCH TO YOUR DISAPPOINTMENT. SKIP ONE TURN.

10

IN A WORLD CUP QUALIFYING GAME THE DEFENSE LEAKS 3 GOALS. GO BACK 3 PLACES.

8

INJURY PREVENTS YOU FROM TAKING PART IN THE NEXT GAME. GO BACK 2 PLACES.

YOU ARE SENT TO THE BENCH IN A FRIENDLY. WARM THE BENCH FOR ONE TURN.

Help the team win!

YOU SCORE FOUR GOALS IN A GAME AGAINST MEXICO. GO FORWARD 4 PLACES.

A FEW TEAMMATES GET LOST WHILE ON THEIR WAY TO A GAME. SKIP ONE TURN.

5

13

YOU SCORE A HAT TRICK IN A GROUP GAME IN THE OLYMPICS. JUMP FORWARD 3 PLACES.

YOU WIN YOUR VERY FIRST INTERNATIONAL GAME. ROLL AGAIN.

YOUR TEAM BEATS BRAZIL AND GOES INTO THE QUARTER-FINAL OF THE OLYMPICS. ROLL AGAIN.

2

THE U.S. WOMEN'S BOARD GAME!

KICKOFF